The Red-headed League

Arthur Conan Doyle

HELBLING LANGUAGES

www.helblinglanguages.com

The Red-headed League
by Arthur Conan Doyle

First published 2007

ISBN 978-3-85272-001-2

The publishers would like to thank the following for their kind permission to reproduce the following photographs and other copyright material: Alamy p 6, p 9.

Series editor and adapted by Maria Cleary
Illustrated by Giulia Sagramola
Activities by Allegra Byrne
Design and layout by Capolinea
Printed by Athesia

About this Book

For the Student

Listen to all of the story and do some activities on your Audio CD

Talk about the story

ink• When you see the orange dot you can check the word in the glossary

For the Teacher

Go to our Readers Resource site for information on using readers and downloadable Resource Sheets, photocopiable Worksheets, Answer Keys and Tapescripts. Plus the full version of the story on MP3.

www.helblinglanguages.com/readers

For lots of great ideas on using Graded Readers consult Reading Matters, the Teacher's Guide to using Helbling Readers.

Level 2 Structures

Past simple of *be*	Comparative
Past simple	Comparative with *as...as*
Past simple (common irregular verbs)	Superlative
Be going to	*To* for purpose
Past Continuous	Adverbs of manner
Past simple v. past continuous	
	A lot of, not much, not many
Past simple in questions	*And, so, but, because*
Have to / Must	Possessive pronouns
Mustn't	

Structures from lower levels are also included.

Contents

About the Author

Arthur Conan Doyle was the inventor of Sherlock Holmes, the world's most famous fictional• detective. Lots of people think Sherlock Holmes is a real person and write to 221b Baker Street, London, his address in Conan Doyle's stories!

Doyle was born in Edinburgh, Scotland in 1859. He worked as a doctor until 1891, when he became a full-time writer. His first story was a novel called *A Study in Scarlet*. He then wrote a series of short stories called *The Adventures of Sherlock Holmes*, which were published in instalments• by *The Strand Magazine*. The public loved them, and wanted to read more about Sherlock Holmes and his faithful friend, Dr. Watson.

Conan Doyle fought in the Boer War (1899-1902) in South Africa, and when he returned to London he was given the title of 'Sir'.

Eventually Conan Doyle became tired of writing about the detective and decided to "kill" his creation. In *The Final Problem* Holmes was murdered by his most dangerous enemy, Professor Moriarty. Conan Doyle's readers were so angry that in the end he was forced to bring Holmes back to life in *The Empty House*.

Arthur Conan Doyle died in 1930. He wrote many books, but most of all he's remembered for his 56 Sherlock Holmes stories, where

Glossary

- **exploits:** actions, adventures
- **fictional:** a person in an invented story is a fictional character
- **instalments:** the story was published in sections. You had to wait for the next edition of the magazine to see what happened next!

he described the exploits of one of the most popular characters in international literature.

The Red-Headed League

Conan Doyle said that *The Red Headed League* was one of his favourite Sherlock Holmes stories. It first appeared in *The Strand Magazine* in August 1891, and is one of the stories in *The Adventures of Sherlock Holmes*, published in 1892.

The story, set in London in 1890, follows Sherlock Holmes and his friend, Dr. Watson, as they attempt to solve the strange puzzle described by a red-headed London pawnbroker, Jabez Wilson. Wilson's employee, Vincent Spaulding, tells him about a group founded by an American millionaire, now dead, who also had red hair. Wilson meets Duncan Ross, the chief of the group, and Ross makes him a strange offer – Wilson can earn a great deal of money simply by spending four hours a day at an office, copying out the *Encyclopaedia Britannica*. He does this for eight weeks, then arrives one day to find the office locked.

He goes to see the great detective. Of course, something much more serious is going on, and Holmes and Watson are soon involved in a fascinating mystery. In this exciting story we see Holmes use reason and logic to defeat the villains John Clay and "Archie".

There's a Sherlock Holmes museum in London. You can visit the website at:
www.sherlock-holmes.co.uk/home

- **attempt:** try
- **great deal of:** a lot of
- **pawnbroker:** someone who lends you money in exchange for something you own. If you don't pay the money back in time, the shopkeeper will sell the item
- **villains:** bad people; criminals

Before Reading

1 The title of the story is "The Red-headed League". What kind of story do you think it is? Why? Ask and answer with a partner.

a) Horror
b) Detective
c) Love
d) Adventure
e) Science fiction

2 Think about the title. The Red-headed League is a:

a) football team
b) club for men with red hair
c) shop selling wigs
d) cruise ship

3 Look at this picture from the book and answer. The story is set in:

a) modern times
b) 18th century
c) the future
d) 19th century

4 **The pictures below show two important characters in the story. Match each picture with the description.**

a) ☐

b) ☐

1) Jabez Wilson is a fat red-faced gentleman with red hair.
2) Sherlock Holmes is a famous detective. He often smokes his pipe.

5 **Find the following words in the story. Match them to their drawings.**

a) coins **b)** crate **c)** earring **d)** stone steps **e)** gipsy

f) Irish setter **g)** labyrinth **h)** pavement **i)** sticks **l)** gate

1 ☐

2 ☐

3 ☐

4 ☐
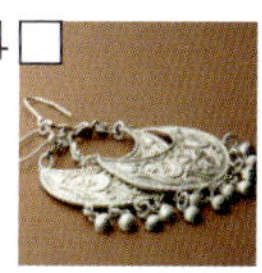

5 ☐

6 ☐

7 ☐
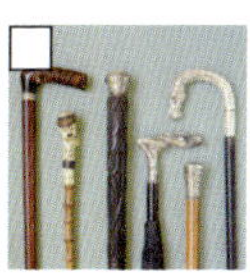

8 ☐

9 ☐

10 ☐

2 When I called on my friend, Mr. Sherlock Holmes, one day in the autumn of last year I found him in deep conversation with a fat, red-faced gentleman with bright red hair•.

"You come at a good time, my dear Watson," he said.
"I was afraid that you were busy."
"I am. Very busy."
"Then I can wait in the next room."
"Not at all•. Meet Mr. Wilson. Mr. Wilson, Dr. Watson is my partner and helper. He helps me in many of my cases•, and I have no doubt that he can help me in yours also."
"Sit down," said Holmes.
"Your cases are always of the greatest interest to me," I said.
"Do you remember what I said the other day? That for strange events we must go to life itself. Because life is always much stranger than the imagination."
"Yes, and I remember I disagreed with you."

Glossary

- **bright red hair:** hair of an orange-red colour
- **cases:** strange events or crimes that policemen solve
- **not at all:** don't do that

"You did, Doctor. Listen to Mr. Jabez Wilson's story and see if you change your mind. Mr. Wilson, can you start your story once more? That way Dr. Watson can hear the opening part and I can hear the details again."

Mr. Wilson puffed out• his chest and pulled a dirty and wrinkled• newspaper from the pocket of his coat. He looked through the advertisements in the newspaper. I studied his appearance.

I did not learn very much from my inspection•. Our visitor looked like an average British working man, fat, arrogant, and slow. He wore baggy• grey trousers, a black coat, unbuttoned in the front, and a drab• waistcoat with a heavy watch-chain. An old top-hat• and a brown overcoat were on the chair beside him. The only remarkable thing about the man was his red head•, and the expression of extreme discontent on his face.

Glossary

- **baggy:** wide; not fitting well
- **drab:** not smart, dull in colour
- **inspection:** careful look
- **puffed out:** made bigger
- **red head:** orange-coloured hair
- **top-hat:** tall hat
- **wrinkled:** with lots of folds and lines

Sherlock Holmes started:

"Obviously he did manual labour, he is a Freemason, he was in China, and he did a lot of writing."
"How do you know all that, Mr. Holmes?" asked Mr. Wilson. "How did you know that I did manual labour? It's true, of course."
"Your hands, my dear sir. Your right hand is much larger than your left hand. You worked hard with it, and the muscles are more developed."
"And the Freemasonry?"
"Elementary, against the rules of the Freemasons, you wear an arc-and-compass breastpin."

"Ah, of course, I forgot that. But the writing?"
"The right cuff of your coat is very shiny, and the left arm has a smooth patch near the elbow where you rested it on a desk."
"And China?"
"The fish tattoo above your right wrist can only come from China. I study tattoos and the delicate pink colour of the fishes' scales is unique to China. And I can see a Chinese coin hanging from your watch-chain. Once more, elementary."

Mr. Jabez Wilson laughed loudly.

"Well, well!" he said. "Elementary."
"I begin to think, Watson," said Holmes, "that I made a mistake in explaining things. 'Unknown things seem important.' Can you not find the advertisement, Mr. Wilson?"
"Yes, I have got it now," he answered with his big red finger pointing halfway down the column. "Here it is. This is what began it all. Read it, sir."

All about Jabez Wilson

How does Sherlock Holmes know that Mr. Jabez Wilson

a did manual labour?
b is a Freemason?
c was in China?
d did a lot of writing?

Glossary

- **cuff:** lower end of a sleeve
- **Freemason:** member of a secret club for men (Freemasonry/Freemasons)
- **manual labour:** low-paid work with your hands (eg digging or building, but not surgery or programming)
- **scales:** (here) small, hard, translucent pieces of skin on a fish's body
- **smooth:** flat
- **tattoo:** (here) a picture or design on someone's skin, made by using needles and inks

I took the paper from him and read as follows:

TO THE RED-HEADED LEAGUE: Thanks to the inheritance of the late Ezekiah Hopkins, of Lebanon, Pennsylvania, U. S. A., there is now another vacancy open for a new member of the Red-headed League. Each member of the League receives a salary of £4 a week for minimum services. All red-headed men who are healthy in body and mind and above the age of twenty-one years, can apply.

Apply in person on Monday, at eleven o'clock, to *Duncan Ross*, at the offices of the League, 7 *Pope's Court, Fleet Street*.

"What on earth does this mean?" I exclaimed after I read the extraordinary advertisement.

Holmes laughed and wriggled• in his chair. "It is a little strange, isn't it?" he said. "And now, Mr. Wilson, tell us all about yourself, your household•, and the effect that this advertisement had on your life. First make a note, Doctor, of the paper and the date."
"It is ***The Morning Chronicle*** of April 27, 1890. Just two months ago."

"Very good. Now, Mr. Wilson?"

The Red-headed League

What is strange about the advertisement?

Invent another league. Who can join it?

Glossary

- **household:** people who live in a house
- **inheritance:** money left to other people when someone dies
- **late:** dead
- **salary:** money paid for work done ('professional' work)
- **wriggled:** made small, quick movements
- **vacancy:** place

"Well, as I told you, Mr. Sherlock Holmes," said Jabez Wilson, touching his forehead, "I have a small shop at Saxe-Coburg Square, near the City•. It's not very large and in recent years it is not very successful. In the past I had two assistants•, now I have one, and I can only pay him because he is willing to• work for half wages• in order to learn the business."

"What is the name of this young man?" asked Sherlock Holmes.

"His name is Vincent Spaulding, and he's not so young, either. It's hard to say his age. I could not have a smarter assistant, Mr. Holmes. I know very well that he could get a better job and earn twice what I give him. But, he is satisfied."

"You are most fortunate in having this employee. It is not a common experience among employers•. Your assistant is as remarkable as your advertisement."

"Oh, he has his faults, too," said Mr. Wilson. "Photography ... taking pictures with his camera then going down into the cellar• like a rabbit into its hole to develop• them. That is his main fault, but he's a good worker. There's no badness in him."

"He is still with you, I presume?"

"Yes, sir. He and a girl of fourteen, who does some cooking and cleaning. That's everyone in the house, because my wife is dead and we didn't have any children. We live very quietly, sir, the three of us.

Glossary

- **assistants:** helpers
- **cellar:** room under a house
- **City:** the business centre of London
- **develop:** make a photograph from a film
- **employers:** people who other people work for
- **wages:** money paid for work done (manual labour)
- **is willing to:** wants to

3 "The first thing that disturbed• us was that advertisement. Spaulding came into the office eight weeks ago, with this paper in his hand, and he said:

" 'I wish, Mr. Wilson, that I was a red-headed man.'

" 'Why?' I asked.

" 'Because,' he said, 'there's another vacancy at the League of Red-headed Men. It's worth a fortune to• the man who gets it, and I understand that there are more vacancies than there are men.'

" 'Why, what is this 'League'?' I asked. You see, Mr. Holmes, I am a very stay-at-home• man. My business comes to me and I am often weeks on end without putting my foot over the door-mat•. So I don't know what is going on outside, and I am always happy to hear some news.

" 'Have you never heard of the League of Red-headed Men?' he asked with his eyes open.

" 'Never.'

" 'Why, that is strange, for you are eligible• for one of the vacancies.'

Glossary

- **disturbed:** changed our routine
- **door-mat:** small carpet in front of the door for cleaning your shoes
- **eligible:** suitable; one of the right people
- **it's worth a fortune to:** there's a lot of money for
- **stay-at-home:** who doesn't go out

" 'And what are they?' I asked.

" 'Oh, each vacancy pays a couple of• hundred pounds a year. But there is little work to do.'

"Well, you can be sure that I was interested. My business was not very successful, and I liked the thought of an extra couple of hundred pounds.

" 'Tell me all about it,' I said.

" 'Well,' he said, showing me the advertisement, 'you can see for yourself that the League has a vacancy. Here is the address where you can apply• for details. The League was founded• by an American millionaire, Ezekiah Hopkins, who was very strange in his ways•. He was red-headed, and he had a great sympathy• for all red-headed men. So, when he died, he left his money to a group of trustees•, with instructions to give the money to men with red hair. It is good pay and there is very little to do.'

" 'But,' I said, 'there are millions of red-headed men who can apply.'

" 'Not as many as you think,' he answered. 'You see it is only for Londoners, and grown men. This American came from London, and he wanted to do something good for the old town. And, I have heard, you can't apply if your hair is light red, or dark red, or anything but real bright, blazing, fiery red. You hair is perfect, Mr. Wilson, if you want to apply. But perhaps it's not worth your while applying for just a couple of hundred pounds.'

What is the Red-headed League?

Why does Ezekiah Hopkins start the Red-Headed League?

What do you need before you can join?

Glossary

- **apply:** ask for a job, usually by writing a letter
- **a couple of:** two
- **founded:** started
- **strange in his ways:** eccentric
- **sympathy:** understanding and support
- **trustees:** group of people who look after money or an inheritance for someone else

"Now, it is a fact, gentlemen, as you may see for yourselves that my hair is a full and rich red. So I decided to apply for the vacancy. I ordered Vincent Spaulding to close the shop for a day and to come with me. He was happy to have a holiday, so we closed the shop and went off to the address in the advertisement.

"Well, Mr. Holmes, from north, south, east, and west every man who had red hair was there to answer the advertisement. Fleet Street and Pope's Court were crowded with red-headed men. There was every shade of red – straw, lemon, orange, brick, Irish-setter; but, as Spaulding said, there were not many with the real vivid flame-coloured red. When I saw all these men I wanted to go away; but Spaulding refused. He pushed and pulled until we moved through the crowd, and right up to the office."

Complete the spider diagram with all the red things you know.

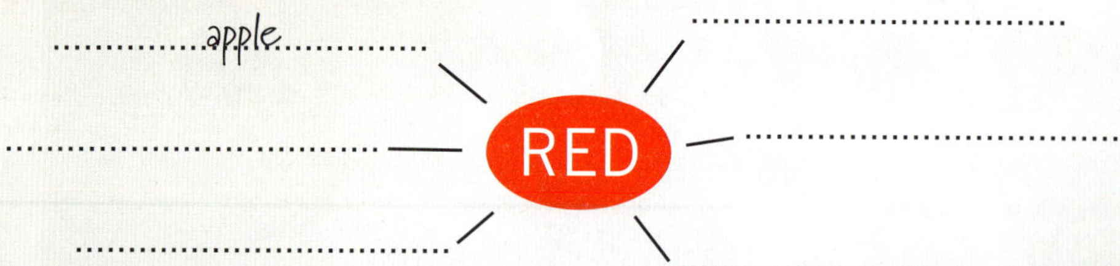

Glossary

- **brick:** rectangular pieces of baked clay, used for building houses, walls etc
- **crowded with:** full of
- **flame-coloured:** like a fire
- **full:** (here) intense
- **Irish-setter:** a breed of dog that has copper-red hair
- **shade:** variation in colour
- **straw:** dried stalks of cereals (wheat, barley etc)

CAFE

"There was nothing in the office but a couple of wooden chairs and a table. A small man with a head that was redder than mine was sitting behind the table. He said a few words to each candidate•, and then he sent them away. Getting a place in the League did not seem to be very easy. However, when it was our turn the little man closed the door so he could have a private word with us.

" 'This is Mr. Jabez Wilson,' my assistant said, 'and he wants to apply for a place in the League.'

" 'And he is perfect for it,' the other answered. 'I cannot remember the last time I saw hair so perfect.' He took a step backwards and looked at my hair until I felt embarrassed. Then suddenly he moved forward, shook my hand, and congratulated me on my success.

" 'The vacancy is yours,' he said. 'Excuse me for taking an obvious precaution•.' And with that he took my hair in both his hands, and pulled until I shouted with the pain. 'There is water in your eyes. Now I know that your hair is real. We have to be careful.' He stepped over to the window and shouted through it at the top of his voice that the vacancy was filled. We heard a groan• of disappointment and the men went away in different directions until there was not one red-head left, except me and the manager.

? Duncan Ross

Why does the manager pull Mr. Jabez Wilson's hair?

Glossary

- **candidate:** person who applies for a job or vacancy
- **groan:** sound people make when they are sad or hurt
- **precaution:** action to prevent something bad or unwanted from happening

" 'My name,' he said, 'is Mr. Duncan Ross, and I am one of the League. Are you a married man, Mr. Wilson? Have you got a family?'

" 'No,' I answered.

" 'Oh dear!' he said, 'that is very serious! The fund hopes to encourage and support red-heads. It is unfortunate that you haven't got any children.'

"I thought that I was not to have the vacancy after all. The man thought for a few minutes and then said that I could join the League.

" 'We cannot refuse a man with hair like yours. When can you start your new duties?'

" 'Well, it is a little awkward, for I have a business already,' I said.

" 'Oh, don't worry about that, Mr. Wilson!' Vincent Spaulding said. 'I can look after the business for you.'

" 'What are the hours?' I asked.

" 'From ten until two.'

"Now I do most of my business in the evening, Mr. Holmes, so it was good for me to earn a little in the mornings. Besides, I knew that my assistant was a good man, and that he would look after the business for me.

Glossary

- **awkward:** difficult
- **fund:** (here) the League

" 'That sounds good,' I said. 'And the pay?'

" 'Is £4 a week.'

" 'And the work?'

" 'Well, you have to be in the office, or at least in the building, for the four hours. If you leave, you lose your place forever. The will is very clear on that point. It says you can't leave the office during that time.'

" 'It's only four hours a day. I'm not going to leave,' I said.

" 'There are no excuses,' Mr. Duncan Ross said; 'You must stay there, or you lose your place in the League.'

" 'And the work?'

" 'Is to copy out the *Encyclopaedia Britannica*. The first volume• of it is in the cupboard. You must bring your own ink•, pen and paper, but we provide• this table and chair. Can you start tomorrow?'

" 'Certainly,' I answered.

Glossary

- **in low spirits:** sad
- **ink:** blue or black liquid that is in pens for writing
- **provide:** give someone what they need
- **volume:** book (usually one in a series of books)

" 'Then, goodbye, Mr. Jabez Wilson, and let me congratulate you once more.' He showed me out of the room and I went home with my assistant. I didn't know what to say or do; I was so pleased at my own good fortune.

"Well, I thought about it all day, and by evening I was in low spirits•.

Think of a time when you were lucky

What happened? What did you do?

Write a paragraph to describe it.

again. I was sure that the whole thing was a joke or trick. Vincent Spaulding tried to cheer me up. However, in the morning I decided to go to the office. I bought a penny bottle of ink, and with a pen, and seven sheets of paper, I walked to Pope's Court.

"Well, to my surprise, everything was fine. The table was ready for me, and Mr. Duncan Ross was there to greet me. He told me to start at the letter A. He left and came from time to time to check that everything was fine. At two o'clock he came back, thanked me and locked the door of the office after me.

"This went on day after day, Mr. Holmes, and on Saturday the manager came in and gave me four golden sovereigns• for my week's work. It was the same the next week, and the same the week after. Every morning I was there at ten, and every afternoon I left at two. Mr. Duncan Ross stopped coming to check me but I didn't leave the room because I didn't want to lose my place in the League.

"Eight weeks passed like this. I wrote about Abbots and Archery and Armour and Architecture and Attica, and hoped to start on the Bs before very long. And then suddenly the whole business came to an end."

"To an end?"

Glossary

- **cheer me up:** make me happy
- **penny bottle of ink:** a bottle of ink that cost one penny
- **sheets:** (here) pieces
- **sovereigns:** gold coins, worth £1 each

"Yes, sir, this morning. I went to my work as usual at ten o'clock, but the door was shut and locked. There was a little square of cardboard• hanging on the door. Here it is, and you can read for yourself."

He held up a piece of white cardboard about the size of a sheet of note-paper•:

> THE RED-HEADED LEAGUE
>
> IS
>
> DISSOLVED•.
>
> October 9, 1890.

Sherlock Holmes and I looked at both the announcement and the sad face behind it. The comical side of the affair• was so obvious that we both burst into laughter.

"I cannot see anything very funny," our client shouted. "I can leave if all you can do is laugh at me."

? Think about what happened

Why do you think Sherlock Holmes and Dr. Watson burst into laughter?

"No, no," cried Holmes, pushing him back into the chair. "I really want to work on your case. It is most unusual. But there is something strange about it. Tell me, what did you do when you found the card on the door?"

"I was shocked, sir. I did not know what to do. Then I called at the other offices in the building, but none of them seemed to know anything about it. Finally, I went to the landlord•, who is an accountant• living on the ground floor, and I asked him about the notice. He knew nothing. Then I asked him about Mr. Duncan Ross. He said that the name was new to him.

" 'Well, he is the gentleman upstairs,' I said.

" 'What, the red-headed man?'

" 'Yes.'

" 'Oh,' he said, 'his name was William Morris. He was a solicitor• and was using the room until his new office was ready. He moved out yesterday.'

" 'Where can I find him?' I asked.

" 'Oh, at his new office,' he replied and told me the address. 17 King Edward Street, near St. Paul's.'

Glossary

- **accountant:** someone who looks after the money in a company
- **affair:** (here) event
- **cardboard:** thick, stiff, heavy paper
- **dissolved:** (here) ended
- **landlord:** person who rents rooms or houses
- **note-paper:** piece of paper used for writing a letter
- **solicitor:** a lawyer who gives legal advice

"I went there, Mr. Holmes, but when I got to that address no one knew either Mr. William Morris or Mr. Duncan Ross."

"And what did you do then?".

"I went home to Saxe-Coburg Square, and spoke to my assistant. But he did not help me in any way. I did not wish to lose my place in the League, so, I decided to come to you for some advice."

"And you did very wisely," said Holmes. "Your case is an exceedingly remarkable one, and I am happy to work on it. From what you say I think that it is more serious than it appears at first sight."

"It *is* serious!" said Mr. Jabez Wilson. "What about my four pounds a week?"

"As far as you are personally concerned," Holmes said, "I do not see that you can complain about this extraordinary league. On the contrary, you are, as I understand, richer by £30. And you learned everything on every subject beginning with the letter A. No, you can't complain."

"No, sir. But I want to find out about them, and who they are, and what their object was in playing this joke – if it was a joke – on me. It was an expensive joke for them, for it cost them two and thirty pounds•."

"We're going to try to do that. But first, one or two questions, Mr. Wilson. This assistant of yours, Vincent Spaulding – when did he start working with you?"

"About a month ago."
"How did you meet him?"
"He answered an advertisement."
"Was he the only applicant?"
"No, there were a dozen."
"Why did you choose him?"
"Because he was cheap."
"Half price, in fact."
"Yes."

Glossary

- **two and thirty pounds:** old-fashioned way of saying 'thirty-two pounds'

"What is he like, this Vincent Spaulding?"
"Small, stout•, very quick in his ways, no hair on his face, though he's at least thirty. He has a white mark on his forehead."

Holmes sat up in his chair in excitement. "I thought so," he said.

"Are his ears pierced• for earrings?"

"Yes, sir. He told me that a gipsy pierced his ears when he was a boy."

"Hum!" said Holmes, deep in thought. "Is he still with you?"

"Oh, yes, sir."

"Did he look after your business when you were working for the League?"

"Yes, sir. There's never very much to do in the morning."

"That's fine, Mr. Wilson. I can tell you more on the subject in a day or two. Today is Saturday. I hope that by Monday we may come to a conclusion."

Who is Vincent Spaulding?

Do you think Sherlock Holmes knows Spaulding? Why?

Glossary

- **pierced:** with a hole in them
- **stout:** fat

4 "Well, Watson," said Holmes when our visitor left us, "what do you think of it all?"

"I don't know," I answered honestly. "It is a most mysterious business."

"As a rule," said Holmes, "the stranger a thing seems the less mysterious it really is. It is your ordinary crimes which are really mysterious, just as an ordinary face is the most difficult to identify. But I must work quickly in this case."

"What are you going to do, then?" I asked.

"To smoke," he answered. "It is a three pipe problem•. Please don't speak to me for fifty minutes." He sat in his chair, with his thin knees drawn up• to his long nose, and there he stayed with his eyes closed and his black pipe sticking out like the bill• of some strange bird. I thought that he was sleeping, and indeed I was falling asleep myself, when he suddenly jumped out of his chair and put his pipe on the mantelpiece•.

"Sarasate• is playing at St. James's Hall this afternoon," he remarked. "What do you think, Watson? Can you leave your patients• for a few hours?"

"I have nothing to do today. My practice• is never very busy."

"Then put on your hat and come. I am going through the City first, and we can have some lunch on the way. Come along!"

We travelled by the Underground• as far as Aldersgate; and walked to Saxe-Coburg Square. A brown board with "JABEZ WILSON" in white letters marked the place where our red-headed client worked and lived. Sherlock Holmes stopped in front of it with his head on one side• and looked carefully at it. Then he walked slowly up the street, and then down again to the corner, still looking closely at the houses. Finally he returned to the shop and hit the pavement with his stick two or three times. Then he went up to the door and knocked. A bright-looking, clean-shaven• young fellow opened the door and asked him to come in.

Glossary

- **bill:** beak; hard part of a bird's mouth
- **clean-shaven:** his facial hair (beard and moustache) carefully and completely removed by shaving
- **drawn up:** pulled up
- **head on one side:** a posture indicating deep thought
- **mantelpiece:** shelf over a fireplace
- **patients:** ill people who consult a doctor
- **practice:** (here) the work of a doctor
- **Sarasate:** Spanish violinist (1844–1908)
- **three pipe problem:** to solve this problem will take enough time for me to smoke three pipes (of tobacco)
- **Underground:** railway train that goes in tunnels beneath the city

"Thank you," said Holmes, "I only wanted to know how to go from here to the Strand."

"Third right, fourth left," answered the assistant and closed the door.

"Smart fellow, that," Holmes said while we were walking away. "I know about him."

"Evidently," I said, "Mr. Wilson's assistant is important in this mystery of the Red-headed League. I am sure that you knocked on the door in order to see him."

"Not him."

"What then?"

"The knees of his trousers."

"And what did you see?"

"What I expected to see."

"Why did you hit the pavement?"

"My dear doctor, let's look, not talk. We are spies in an enemy's country. Let us now explore the area behind Saxe-Coburg Square."

The road behind Saxe-Coburg Square was a main road. It was as different to Saxe-Coburg Square as the front of a picture is different to the back. "Let me see," Holmes said, standing at the corner and looking down the road. "I want to remember the order of the houses here. There is Mortimer's, the tobacconist, the little newspaper shop, the Bank, the Vegetarian Restaurant, and McFarlane's Carriages. And now, Doctor, that's enough. Let's have a sandwich and a cup of coffee, and then off to our concert."

Answer the question

What do you think Sherlock Holmes expected to see?

Glossary

- **carriages:** vehicles pulled by horses
- **main:** important
- **off to our concert:** let's go to the concert that we have planned to attend
- **smart:** clever; intelligent
- **third right, fourth left:** take the third street on the right, then the fourth street on the left

All afternoon my friend sat in the most perfect happiness, gently moving his long, thin fingers in time to the music.

"You want to go home, no doubt, Doctor," he said as we left the concert.

"Yes, indeed."

"And I have some work to do. This business at Saxe-Coburg Square is serious."

"Why serious?"

"A serious crime is going to take place. I believe we can stop it. I am going to need your help tonight."

"At what time?"

"Ten is early enough. And, I say, Doctor, it may be dangerous, so please put your army revolver in your pocket." He waved his hand and disappeared in an instant among the crowd.

Now, I am not more stupid than other people but when I work with Sherlock Holmes I always feel immensely stupid. He always seemed to understand what was happening. As I drove home to my house in Kensington I tried to work out the mysteries of the day but the whole business was still confused to me.

It was a quarter-past nine when I left my home and walked across the Park, and down Oxford Street to Baker Street. Two cab drivers were standing at the door. I went in and I heard the sound of voices

upstairs. Holmes was in animated conversation with two men. One of them was Peter Jones, a well-known policeman.
"Ta! Our party• is complete," said Holmes "Watson, I think you know Mr. Jones, of Scotland Yard•. Let me introduce you to Mr. Merryweather, our companion• in tonight's adventure."
"We're hunting in pairs again, Doctor, you see," Jones said. "Our friend here is a wonderful man for starting a chase."

Glossary

- **cab:** taxi
- **in an instant:** immediately
- **no doubt:** I am sure
- **party:** (here) group of people
- **revolver:** type of hand gun
- **work out:** understand
- **companion:** someone who accompanies you
- **Scotland Yard:** the head office of the British police force in London

"I hope a wild goose is not at the end of our chase," Mr. Merryweather said sadly.

"No, Mr. Merryweather, We are chasing John Clay, the murderer, thief and forger. He's a young man, Mr. Merryweather, but he is at the top of his profession. He's a remarkable man. His grandfather was a royal duke. He went to school at Eton and Oxford. He is very clever and though we see signs of him everywhere, we never know where to find him," Jones explained.

"I agree with you that he is at the top of his profession," Sherlock Holmes said. "It is after ten, it's time to go. You two take the first cab, Watson and I can follow you in the second one."

Sherlock Holmes was not very communicative during the long drive. We drove through a labyrinth of streets until we came to Farrington Street.

"We are close now," my friend said. "Merryweather is a bank director, and personally interested in the matter•. I asked Jones to come with us also. He is not a bad fellow•, though an absolute imbecile• in his profession. He has some good points. He is brave and determined. Here we are. They are waiting for us."

We were in the same busy street as this morning. We followed Mr. Merryweather down a narrow passage• and through a side door. We went down a small corridor, which ended in a massive iron• gate. Merryweather opened the gate and went down some stone steps. He opened another gate and led us down a dark passage. He then opened a third door and went into a large cellar full of crates and boxes.

What is a 'wild goose chase'?

a ☐ traditional British hunting sport.
b ☐ useless search for something you can never find.
c ☐ shopping trip.

Glossary

- **duke:** a top-rank nobleman
- **Eton:** an elite boys' school
- **forger:** someone who makes false copies of money or documents
- **imbecile:** very stupid person
- **iron:** heavy metal
- **matter:** the event; the affair; what we are doing
- **not a bad fellow:** a nice person
- **Oxford:** (here) the university
- **passage:** footpath between buildings
- **ten:** (here) ten o'clock in the evening

Mr. Merryweather hit the floor with his stick. "Dear me, it sounds quite hollow!" he said in surprise.

"I must ask you to be quiet!" said Holmes severely. "Now sit down upon one of these boxes, and please be quiet!"

Mr. Merryweather sat on a crate while Holmes began to examine the cracks on the floor with a magnifying lens.

"We have at least an hour before us," he said, "for they must wait until Mr. Wilson is safely in bed. We are at present, Doctor, in the cellar of one of the most important banks in London. Mr. Merryweather is the chairman of directors of the bank. Mr. Merryweather, tell Dr. Watson why John Clay is interested in this cellar."

"It is our French gold," whispered the director.

"Your French gold?"

"Yes. Some months ago we borrowed 30,000 coins from the Bank of France. The money is still in our cellar. The crate I am sitting on contains 2,000 coins. We have much more gold at present than is usually kept in a single bank."

"Now it is time we made our little plans." Sherlock Holmes said. "Mr. Merryweather, we must cover the light in your lantern."

"And sit in the dark?"

"I am afraid so. We cannot risk the presence of a light. First of all, we must choose our positions. These are dangerous men and we must be careful. Let's hide behind the crates. Then, when I flash a light on the criminals, surround them quickly. If they shoot, Watson, please return fire• at once."

I placed my revolver on top of the wooden crate beside me. Holmes covered his lantern and left us in the dark.

Glossary

- **at present:** now
- **borrowed:** took something that belonged to someone else (usually with their permission), intending to return it
- **cracks:** lines where the floor is broken
- **Dear me:** an old-fashioned exclamation indicating surprise
- **hollow:** empty
- **magnifying lens:** a glass you hold that makes things look bigger
- **return fire:** shoot back at someone who shoots at you
- **severely:** in a strict way

"They have only one way to escape," whispered Holmes. "That is back through the house into Saxe-Coburg Square. I hope that you have done what I asked you, Jones."

"Yes, I have an inspector and two officers• waiting at the front door."

"Then we have closed all the holes. And now we must be silent and wait."

What a long time it seemed! We waited for an hour and a quarter, but it seemed to me to be much longer. I was tired and stiff•, but I was afraid to change my position. I could hear the gentle breathing of my companions. From my position I looked over the crate in the direction of the floor. Suddenly my eyes saw a light.
At first it was only a small light on the stone floor. Then it became a yellow line, and then, without any warning or sound, a hole opened and a hand appeared in the centre of the little area of light. For a minute or more the hand pointed up through the floor. Then it disappeared and all was dark again except the small light between the stones.
Then there was a loud sound and one of the big, white stones turned

Think back

Go back to page 42. Why do you think Sherlock Holmes looked at the man's knees and hit the pavement?

over upon its side and left a square hole. A clean-cut•, boyish• face looked out of the hole. He climbed out and was soon standing at the side of the hole. He then helped his companion, a small man, with a pale• face and lots of very red hair.

Glossary

- **boyish:** like a boy
- **clean-cut:** looking neat and clean
- **officers:** ordinary policemen
- **pale:** white
- **stiff:** finding it difficult and painful to move

"It's all clear," he whispered. "Have you got everything? Great Scott•! Escape, Archie, escape!"

Sherlock Holmes jumped out and held the intruder• by the collar•. The other jumped down the hole. The light flashed on a revolver, but Holmes' stick came down on the man's wrist, and the pistol• fell onto the stone floor.

"It's no use, John Clay," said Holmes. "You have no chance at all."

"So I see," the other answered. "I imagine• that my friend is all right."

"There are three men waiting for him at the door," said Holmes.

"Oh, indeed! I must congratulate you."

"And I you," Holmes answered. "Your red-headed idea was very new and effective."

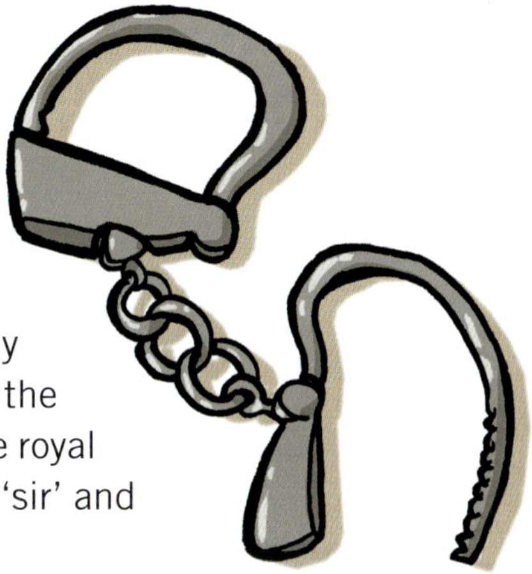

Jones got the handcuffs.

"Please do not touch me with your dirty hands," our prisoner said as Jones fixed the handcuffs on his wrists. "Remember I have royal relations. When you talk to me always say 'sir' and 'please.' "

"All right," said Jones with a smile. "Please, sir, march upstairs, where we can get a cab to bring Your Highness to the police station."

"That is better," said John Clay serenely. And he walked quietly off with the detective.

How do Sherlock Holmes and John Clay treat each other?

a ☐ With anger
b ☐ With fear
c ☐ With respect

Glossary

- **collar:** neck-part of a shirt or coat
- **effective:** with good results
- **Great Scott:** exclamation of surprise
- **handcuffs:** 
- **imagine:** (here) believe; hope
- **intruder:** person who illegally enters a place
- **pistol:** type of hand gun

"Really, Mr. Holmes," said Mr. Merryweather as we followed them from the cellar, "I do not know how the bank can thank you or repay you."

"My pleasure," said Holmes. "The bank can pay some small expenses but I must say I am well repaid by hearing the very remarkable story of the Red-Headed League."

"You see, Watson," he said later in Baker Street. "It was perfectly obvious from the start that the only explanation for the Red-Headed League was to get Mr. Jabez Wilson out of his shop for a number of hours every day. It was a strange way of doing it. But I can't think of a better one. Clay no doubt got the idea from the colour of his accomplice's hair. The £4 a week was not much for them because they hoped to steal thousands. They put the advertisement in the paper. One of them rented the office, and the other one encouraged our man to apply for it. When I heard that the assistant was working for half wages, it was obvious to me that he had some strong reason for wanting the job."

"But how did you guess what the reason was?"

"Well, there were no women in the house so there was no romantic reason. Jabez Wilson is not rich, so stealing from him was not a reason. What could it be? I thought of the assistant's hobby of photography, and his habit of disappearing into the cellar. The cellar was a clue! When I made enquiries into this mysterious assistant I discovered he was one of the most daring criminals in London. I realised that he was doing something in the cellar – something which took many hours a day for a number of months. What could it be? He was digging a tunnel to some other building!

"When we visited Jabez Wilson's shop I hit the pavement with my stick. I wanted to discover if the tunnel was in front of or behind the house. It was not in front of it. Then I rang the bell, and, as I hoped, the assistant answered it. I didn't look at his face. I wanted to see the knees of his trousers. They were dirty and worn• because he had to kneel on the ground in order to dig the tunnel. Now where did the tunnel lead? I walked round the corner, saw the City and Suburban Bank behind our friend's shop, and felt that I had the answer to my question. Then when you drove home after the concert I went to visit Scotland Yard and the chairman of the bank directors."

"And how did you know they were going to make their attempt• tonight?" I asked.

Help Holmes

How did Sherlock Holmes know that Clay and Archie were going to try to rob the bank that night?

Glossary

- **accomplice:** someone who helps you in a crime
- **clue:** something, or some information, that helps solve a crime (or a puzzle)
- **daring:** audacious; who does dangerous and shocking things
- **made enquiries:** asked about
- **make their attempt:** try to do something
- **rented:** paid money to stay in a house or office
- **repay:** do something to thank someone
- **worn:** old and used

"Well, when they dissolved the League, that was a sign that the tunnel was ready. They needed to use it soon, before the bank discovered the tunnel or removed• the gold. Saturday was better than any other day, because the bank was closed and they had two days for their escape. For all these reasons I expected them to come tonight."

"You reasoned it out• beautifully," I said in admiration.

"It stopped me from getting bored•," he answered, yawning•. "These little problems help me to escape the boredom of everyday life."

Glossary

- **bored:** tired and not interested in what is happening
- **reasoned it out:** discovered the answer by logical thinking
- **removed:** took away
- **yawning:** opening your mouth very wide when tired, or before sleeping

After Reading

Personal Response

1 Read each statement and circle the number that is most true for you.

1 = absolutely not
5 = very much

a) I liked the story.	1	2	3	4	5
b) I had no problems in understanding the story.	1	2	3	4	5
c) I have learnt new words.	1	2	3	4	5
d) I would recommend the book to a friend.	1	2	3	4	5

2 Were you surprised by the end of the story? Did you expect it? Why/why not?

3 Sherlock Holmes is one of the most famous fictional detectives. Why is he always able to solve difficult cases? What is unusual about him?

After Reading

Comprehension

1 Are the following sentences true (T) or false (F)? Tick.

		T	F
a)	The narrator is Holmes' partner and friend.	☐	☐
b)	Mr. Wilson comes from China.	☐	☐
c)	The Red-headed League is a league for men with red hair.	☐	☐
d)	Mr. Wilson's shop is big and busy.	☐	☐
e)	He is unhappy with his assistant, Vincent Spaulding.	☐	☐
f)	The assistant wants to apply for the Red-headed League.	☐	☐
g)	Mr. Wilson manages to get a place in the League.	☐	☐
h)	Mr. Wilson has to work from ten to two every day.	☐	☐
i)	One day Mr. Wilson finds out that the League has been dissolved.	☐	☐
j)	Nobody knew Mr. Duncan Ross, the man who offered Mr. Wilson the place in the league.	☐	☐
k)	Holmes thinks Mr. Wilson is a liar.	☐	☐
l)	Vincent Spaulding is friends with John Clay the murderer.	☐	☐
m)	Holmes suspects a bank robbery is going to take place.	☐	☐
n)	Holmes, Watson and one other man wait for the thieves in a cellar under the bank.	☐	☐
o)	At the end the thieves – Vincent and Mr Duncan Ross – are arrested.	☐	☐

2 Choose the correct answers.

a) Mr. Wilson is a

1 ☐ detective.

2 ☐ shop keeper.

3 ☐ thief.

b) Mr Wilson is interested in the vacancy because he wants to

1 ☐ meet other people with red hair.

2 ☐ copy the *Encyclopaedia Britannica*.

3 ☐ earn extra money.

c) Vincent Spaulding invented the Red-headed League because he wanted

1 ☐ to keep Mr. Wilson away from the shop for a few hours every day.

2 ☐ to take pictures with his camera at any time.

3 ☐ to leave his job and work in a bank.

3 *The Red-headed League* is a detective story. Find the clues which lead Sherlock Holmes to suspect Vincent Spaulding, Mr. Wilson's assistant.

a) ....

b) ....

c) ....

d) ....

4 Holmes suspects that the robbery will take place on Saturday. Write down the reasons he gives to support the idea.

After Reading

Characters

1 The main character of the story is Sherlock Holmes. He solves the case at the end. What other characters are there in the story? What do they do? Why are they important to the story?

2 Choose words from the box to describe each character. Write sentences and share with a partner.

a) Sherlock Holmes
b) Dr. Watson
c) Mr. Jabez
d) Vincent Spaulding
e) Mr. Jones
f) John Clay

clever	stupid	shocked	brave	thoughtful	inquisitive
arrogant	discontented	busy	determined	confused	slow
smart					

3 The narrator of the story is Sherlock Holmes' friend, Dr. Watson. How do you see Watson? Circle three adjectives that best describe him throughout the story. Add other adjectives if you want.

bossy	greedy	active	intelligent	lazy	generous
confused	inefficient	helpful	sympathetic	determined	embarrassed
shy	wise	slow			

4 The story is about an attempt to rob a bank. Imagine you are the thief, Vincent Spaulding/John Clay. Describe your plan throughout the following stages.

a) You get a job in Jabez Wilson's small shop.
b) You become so interested in photography.
c) You invented the Red-headed League.
d) You convince Jabez Wilson to apply for a vacancy at the League.
e) You offer to look after the shop when he is away.
f) You dissolve the League.
g) You decide the day of the robbery.

5 The story is a traditional detective story. How is the character of Sherlock Holmes described? What does he like doing? How is his genius described?

6 Imagine you are travelling on the train with Sherlock Holmes. What questions do you ask him?

After Reading

Plot and theme

1 Which comes first? Put the events in the right order.

1	2	3	4	5	6	7	8	9	10	11	12
I											**e**

a) Sherlock Holmes enquires about Wilson's assistant and then he goes to look at the shop.

b) Mr. Wilson applies for the job.

c) Mr. Wilson asks Holmes to help him solve a problem concerning the Red-headed League.

d) He discovers Vincent Spaulding is a criminal and his real name is John Clay.

e) The thieves are arrested.

f) Dr. Watson visits his friend Sherlock Holmes and meets a man with bright red hair and a strange story, Mr. Jabez Wilson.

g) They wait until Wilson's assistant and his companion come out of the hole in the floor.

h) After 8 weeks the League is dissolved and Mr. Duncan Ross disappears.

i) Jabez Wilson's job at the League is to copy out the *Encyclopaedia Britannica*.

j) Sherlock Holmes suspects a serious crime is going to take place so he calls Mr. Jones of Scotland Yard and Mr. Merryweather, a bank director.

k) Holmes and his companions go though a narrow passage, leading to the cellar of one of the most important banks in London.

l) Vincent Spaulding shows Jabez Wilson an advertisement for a vacancy in the Red-headed League.

2 Tell the story in your own words.

3 Imagine you are Dr. Watson. Write a letter to a friend describing what has happened and your feelings about the whole story.

4 At the beginning of the story Sherlock Holmes says:
"For strange events we must go to life itself. Because life is always much stranger than imagination".
What do you think he means? Give your personal interpretation.

5 What are the themes of the story? Discuss in groups and think of situations you have experienced where the classic contrast between good and evil leads to the victory of the former.